HOW TO USE

CANVA

TO DESIGN LIKE A PRO

EDWARD P. ROBINSON

"Design is not just what it looks like and feels like. Design is how it works."
- Steve Jobs

COPYRIGHT

TABLE OF CONTENTS

INTRODUCTION

Welcome to "How To Use Canva To Design Like a Pro". In today's digital age, the ability to create captivating visual content is more crucial than ever. Whether you're a business owner, marketer, student, or simply someone who wants to enhance their creative skills, mastering a versatile design tool like Canva can elevate your projects to the next level.

In this book, we'll dive into the world of Canva, a user-friendly graphic design platform that empowers individuals to bring their ideas to life with ease. From creating eye-catching social media graphics to designing professional presentations and everything in between, Canva offers a plethora of features and templates to suit your needs.

Our journey will begin with an overview of Canva's interface and basic functionalities, ensuring that even beginners can navigate the platform effortlessly. As we progress, we'll explore advanced design techniques, tips, and tricks to help you unleash your creativity and produce stunning visuals that leave a lasting impression.

Throughout this book, you'll find practical step-by-step tutorials, real-world examples, and insightful strategies to help you maximize Canva's potential and create designs that stand out in today's crowded digital landscape. Whether you're looking to boost your business's online presence, create engaging content for your personal projects, or simply hone your design skills, this book will serve as your comprehensive guide to mastering Canva.

So, whether you're a seasoned designer or a novice enthusiast, grab your creativity by the reins and join us on this exciting journey to unleash the full potential of Canva. Get ready to elevate your visual storytelling and design like a pro!

WHAT IS CANVA?

Canva is a graphic design platform that allows users to create a wide range of visual content, including social media graphics, presentations, posters, flyers, and more, without the need for extensive design experience or software expertise. It offers a user-friendly interface, drag-and-drop functionality, and a vast library of templates, images, icons, and fonts to help users create professional-looking designs quickly and easily.

Canva is important for several reasons:

1. **Accessibility**: Canva democratizes design by making it accessible to everyone, regardless of their design background or skill level. It empowers individuals and businesses to create high-quality visual content without the need for expensive software or professional designers.

2. **Efficiency**: With Canva's intuitive interface and pre-designed templates, users can create eye-catching designs in minutes, saving time and effort compared to traditional design methods.

3. **Versatility**: Canva offers a wide range of design options, from social media graphics to presentations to marketing materials. Its versatility makes it suitable for various purposes

and industries, from small businesses and startups to educators and non-profit organizations.

4. **Collaboration**: Canva allows for seamless collaboration between team members or clients, enabling real-time editing, commenting, and sharing of designs. This makes it ideal for collaborative projects and remote work environments.

5. **Cost-effectiveness:** While Canva offers a premium subscription (Canva Pro) with additional features and benefits, the basic version is free to use, making it an affordable option for individuals and organizations with limited budgets.

Overall, Canva simplifies the design process, enabling users to create visually appealing content that effectively communicates their message and enhances their brand identity.

Its accessibility, efficiency, versatility, collaboration features, and cost-effectiveness make it an indispensable tool for anyone looking to create professional-quality designs.

GETTING STARTED

For Mobile Devices:

iOS (iPhone/iPad):

- Access the App Store on your iOS device.
- Use the search icon positioned at the bottom of the screen.
- Input "Canva" into the search field.
- Identify the genuine Canva app from the search results.
- Tap on the app icon, then proceed to select the "Download" option (or the

cloud icon with an arrow if previously installed).
- Confirm the download by entering your Apple ID password or utilizing Touch ID/Face ID.

Android:

- Launch the Google Play Store on your Android device.
- Select the search bar at the top.
- Enter "Canva" and hit enter.
- Locate the authentic Canva app within the search results.
- Tap on the app icon, then choose "Install."
- Wait for the installation process to finish.

After successfully downloading and installing the Canva app on your device, you can begin to explore its functionalities and craft visually engaging designs anytime, anywhere.

For Desktop (Windows/Mac):
- Canva also offers a web version that you can access through your web browser. Simply go to the Canva website and log in or sign up if you haven't already. For a more seamless experience on a desktop, you can use the Canva website without the need for a separate app.

- To access Canva's website, start by opening your preferred web browser. Whether it's Chrome, Firefox, Safari, or another browser, make sure it's up-to-date for the best performance. Find the browser icon either on your desktop or in your applications menu.

- In the address bar located at the top of your browser window, type "www.canva.com" and then press "Enter" on your keyboard.
- Alternatively, you can utilize a search engine to search for "Canva" and click on the official website link displayed in the search results.

To sign up and log in to Canva:

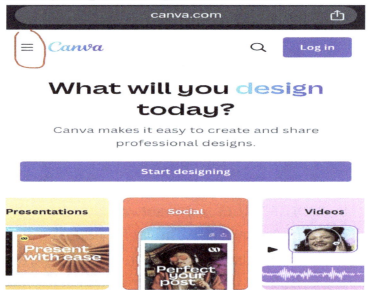

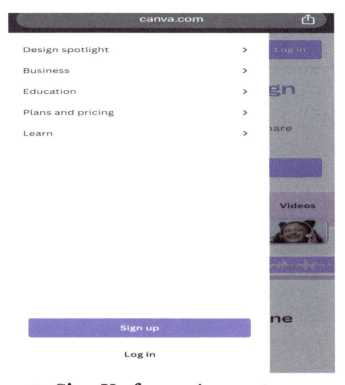

➤ Sign Up for an Account:

- If you're new to Canva, click on the "Sign up" button.
- If you select the email option, provide a valid email address and create a password for your Canva account. Alternatively, use the "*Continue with Google*" or "*Continue with Facebook*" options for faster registration.

- Verify your email address by clicking on the confirmation link sent to your inbox if you signed up using your email.
- Complete your profile by adding your name and any additional details you wish to share. This step is optional but can help personalize your Canva experience.
- Follow the prompts to complete the sign-up process, which may include providing a password and agreeing to Canva's terms of service.

➢ **Log In to Your Account:**
- If you already have a Canva account, click on the "Log in" button.
- Enter the email address and password associated with your Canva account.
- Alternatively, you can log in using your Google or Facebook account if you signed up with those credentials.
- Once logged in, you'll have access to your Canva account dashboard, where

you can start creating designs, explore templates, access your previous designs, and more.

Remember to keep your login credentials secure and to log out of your Canva account when using a shared or public device to ensure the security of your account.

Well done!
You've completed the process of creating your Canva account.
Now, you're all set to unleash your creativity and begin designing.

EXPLORE CANVA INTERFACE

When you first log in to Canva, you'll be greeted by its user-friendly interface, designed to make your design experience smooth and intuitive.

Dashboard Overview:

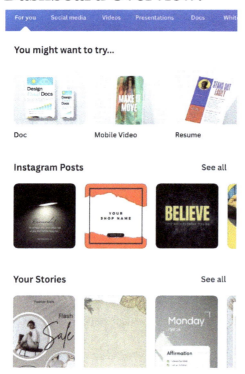

Here's a breakdown of the main components of Canva's interface:

1. Header:
- Located at the top of the screen, the header contains the Canva logo on the left and various navigation options on the right.
- Navigation options include tabs for Home, Create a design, Templates, Photos, Elements, Text, and more.

2. Home Tab:
- The Home tab displays your recent designs and provides suggestions based on your activity.
- You can quickly access your most frequently used templates and designs from this tab.

3. Create a Design Tab:
- Clicking on the "Create a design" or 'plus sign' tab allows you to start a new

design from scratch with custom dimensions.

- You can enter specific dimensions for your design or choose from popular presets such as social media posts, presentations, posters, and more.

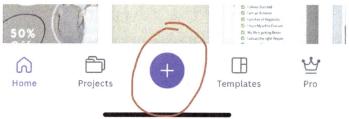

4. Templates Tab:

The Templates tab offers a vast library of pre-designed templates for various purposes.

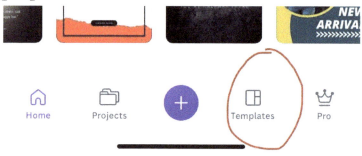

Templates are categorized by type (e.g., social media, marketing, education) and are fully customizable to suit your needs.

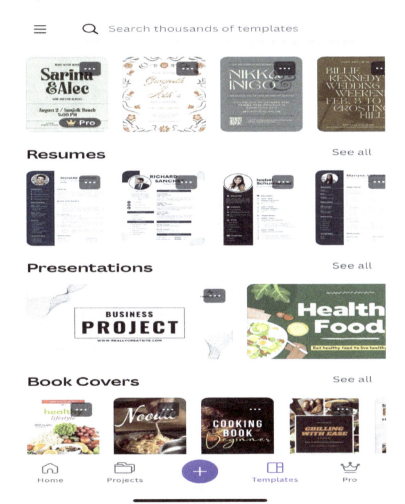

Canva intelligently suggests templates based on your previous designs and popular trends. These recommendations appear on the dashboard, providing inspiration for your next project.

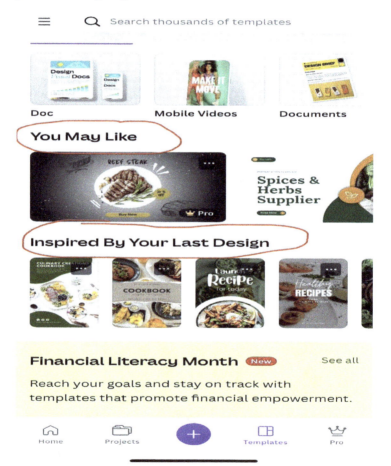

5. Photos Tab:

- The Photos tab provides access to Canva's extensive library of stock images.
- You can search for images by keyword or browse through categories such as nature, business, technology, and more.
- Additionally, you can upload your own images from your computer or device.

6. Elements Tab:

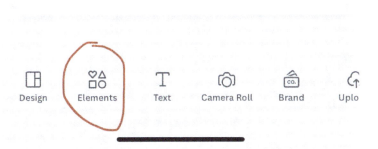

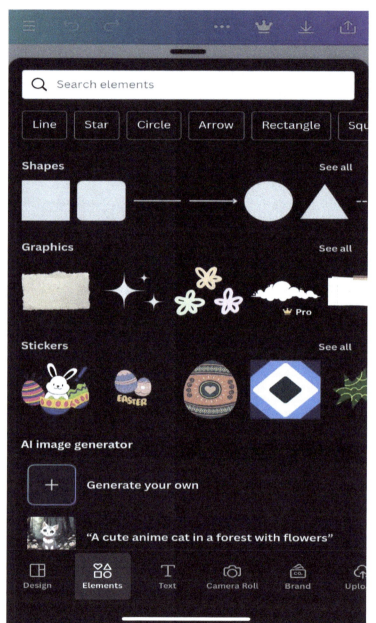

The Elements tab offers a wide range of graphic elements such as icons, shapes, illustrations, and stickers.
These elements can be added to your design to enhance its visual appeal and convey your message effectively.

7. Text Tab:

The Text tab provides options for adding and customizing text in your designs.

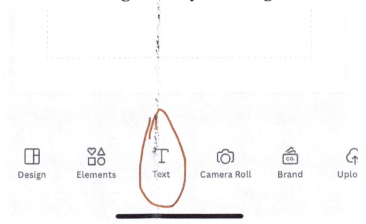

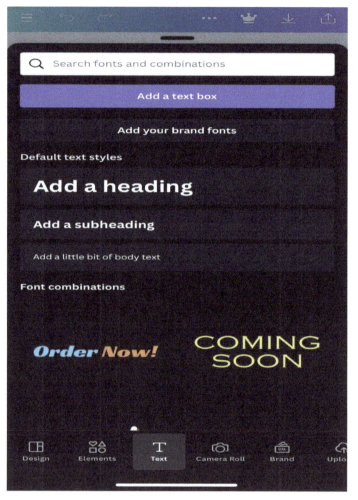

You can choose from a variety of text styles, fonts, sizes, colors, and alignment options to create visually appealing text elements.

GETTING CANVA PRO FOR FREE

Canva Pro is a subscription-based service that offers additional features and benefits compared to the free version of Canva. However, there are a few ways you may be able to access Canva Pro for free:

1. Chrome:
- Open your chrome browser
- On the search bar, type "bingotingo" or click on the link https://bingotingo.com/

- Click on the link to take you to the features. Scroll down to select the image "how to use Kenba"

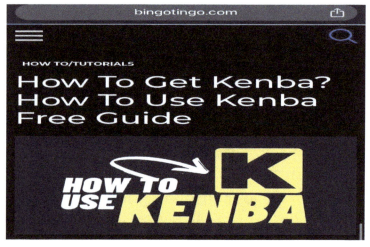

- Scroll down to 'free guide' and wait for the countdown to count to zero.

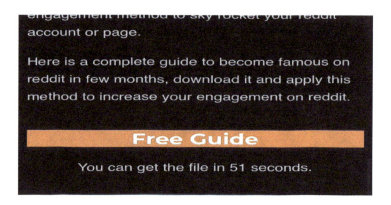

- After the countdown, you will see the download icon, then click on it.

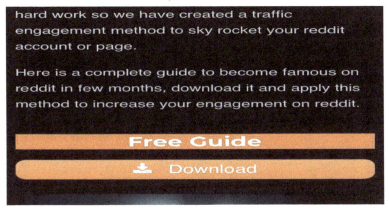

- Next is to click on "get here" and this will take you to the Canva app and join the team automatically.

jaspertucker

GET HERE

FOR FREE SEO TOOLS

SPONSORED BY BINGOTINGO

Congratulations! You can now use the Canva pro for free as long as you join the team.

2. Free Trial:

- Canva often offers a free trial period for Canva Pro, typically ranging from 7 to 30 days.
- You can sign up for a free trial by visiting the Canva website and selecting the Canva Pro subscription option. Keep in mind that you'll need to provide payment information, and you'll be automatically charged for a subscription at the end of the trial period unless you cancel.

3. Education Program:

- Canva offers a free Canva Pro subscription to eligible students and teachers through its Education program.
- To access Canva Pro for free as a student or teacher, you'll need to sign up for Canva using your school email address or verify your status through Canva's Education verification process.

4. Nonprofit Program:

- Canva also offers free Canva Pro subscriptions to eligible nonprofit organizations through its Nonprofit program.
- Nonprofit organizations can apply for Canva Pro access by providing proof of their nonprofit status and completing the application process.

5. Affiliate Programs or Promotions:

- Keep an eye out for special promotions, referral programs, or affiliate partnerships that may offer opportunities to access Canva Pro for free or at a discounted rate.
- Some websites, influencers, or companies may offer Canva Pro giveaways or promotions as part of their marketing efforts.

6. Partnerships with Organizations or Institutions:

- Some organizations, companies, or institutions may have partnerships or agreements with Canva that provide free or discounted access to Canva Pro for their members or employees. Check with your organization or institution to see if such opportunities are available.

Before signing up for any free trial or promotion, be sure to review the terms and conditions carefully to understand any potential charges or limitations associated with the offer. Additionally, keep in mind that availability and eligibility criteria for free access to Canva Pro may vary over time and by region.

SUBSCRIBING TO CANVA PRO

Consider upgrading to Canva Pro for additional features, premium elements, and advanced collaboration options.

- Once you've decided to subscribe to Canva Pro, click on the "Upgrade to Canva Pro" button or navigate to the Canva Pro subscription page. You can typically find the upgrade option in the Canva dashboard or settings menu.

- **Choose a Subscription Plan:** Canva offers different subscription plans for individuals, teams, and enterprises.
- Select the subscription plan that best fits your needs and budget. Plans may vary in terms of features, pricing, and billing frequency (e.g., monthly or annual).

- Review the pricing details and any available discounts or promotions before proceeding.

- **Enter Payment Information:**Provide the required payment information to complete the subscription process.
- You'll need to enter your credit card details or use an alternative payment method accepted by Canva.
- If you're eligible for a free trial, you may need to provide payment information upfront, but you won't be charged until the trial period ends.

- **Review and Confirm:** Review your subscription details, including the selected plan, billing frequency, and payment information, to ensure everything is accurate.
- Confirm your subscription by clicking on the appropriate button (e.g., "Start Your Free Trial" or "Subscribe Now").

- **Access Canva Pro Features:**Once your subscription is confirmed, you'll gain access to Canva Pro features and benefits.
- Log in to your Canva account to start using Canva Pro, and enjoy enhanced design capabilities, premium content, and other perks available exclusively to Canva Pro subscribers.

CHOOSING TEMPLATES

In the Templates tab, you'll find various categories of templates organized by type and purpose.

- Browse through the categories to find templates for social media, presentations, posters, flyers, invitations, and more.

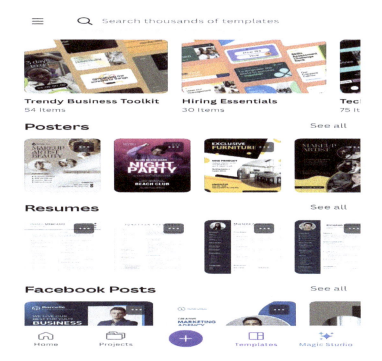

- **Search for Specific Templates**: If you have a specific type of design in mind, use the search bar at the top of the Templates tab to enter keywords related to your project. For example, you can search for "Instagram post," "business card," "wedding invitation," or any other specific design type.

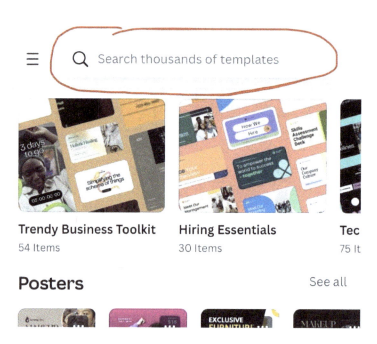

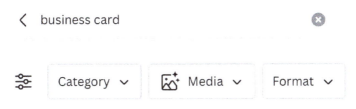

| ⚙ | Category ∨ | 🖼 Media ∨ | Format ∨ |

15,263 templates

+

Create blank

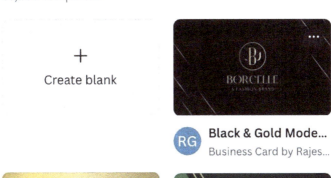

RG **Black & Gold Mode...**
Business Card by Rajes...

 **Gold Elegant and M...**
Business Card by Rayh...

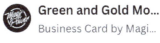 **Green and Gold Mo...**
Business Card by Magi...

- **Preview Templates:** Click on a template category or search result to view the available templates within that category. Scroll through the

39

templates to preview different designs and layouts.

- **Select a Template:** Once you've found a template that suits your needs, click on it to select it. The template will open in the editor, where you can customize it to fit your branding, message, and preferences.

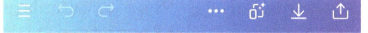

KIMBERLY NGUYEN

Ramen House

123 Anywhere St. Any City

hello@reallygreatsite.com

+123-456-7890

1   +   2   +

Design

Elements

T
Text

Camera Roll

Brand

Uplo

- **Customize Your Template:** Customize the selected template by replacing placeholder text, images, and elements with your own content.

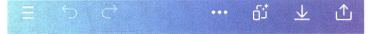

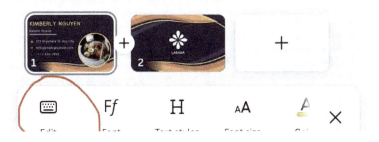

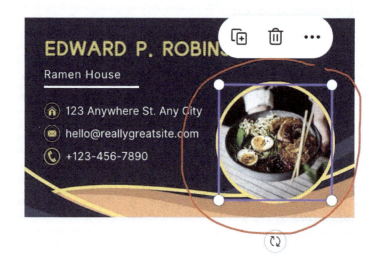

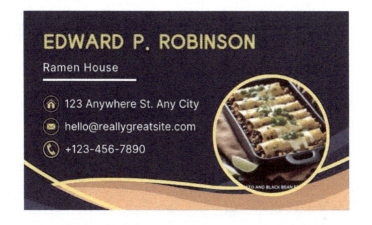

EDWARD P. ROBINSON

Ramen House

🏠 123 Anywhere St. Any City

✉ hello@reallygreatsite.com

📞 +123-456-7890

- Use Canva's editing tools and features to modify colors, fonts, sizes, layouts, and other design elements as desired.

- **Save and Download Your Design:** Once you've customized the template to your liking, click on the "Download" button to save it to your computer or device.

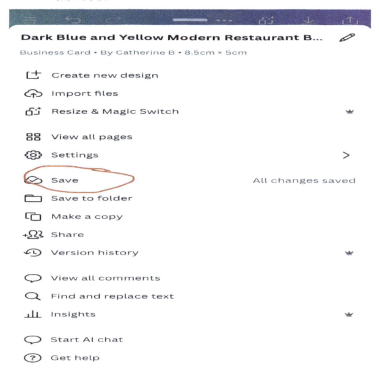

Dark Blue and Yellow Modern Restaurant B...
Business Card • By Catherine B • 8.5cm × 5cm

- Create new design
- Import files
- Resize & Magic Switch
- View all pages
- Settings　　　　　　　　　>
- Save　　　　　　　All changes saved
- Save to folder
- Make a copy
- Share
- Version history
- View all comments
- Find and replace text
- Insights
- Start AI chat
- Get help

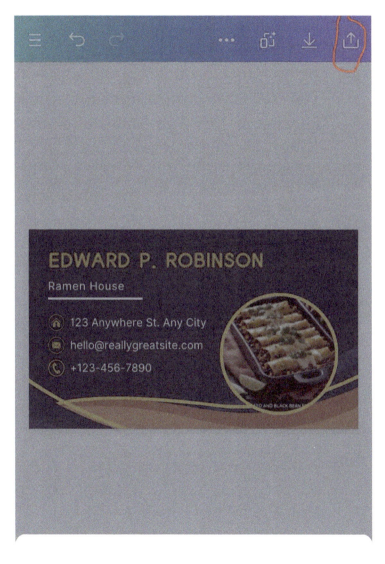

EDWARD P. ROBINSON

Ramen House

🏠 123 Anywhere St. Any City

✉ hello@reallygreatsite.com

📞 +123-456-7890

Invite   Public view link   Template link   Present   Clipbo

↓ Download

⌇ Share link   Suggested

- Choose the desired file format (e.g., PNG, JPG, PDF) and quality settings before downloading. You can also save your design to your Canva account by clicking on the "Save" button to access it later or make further edits.

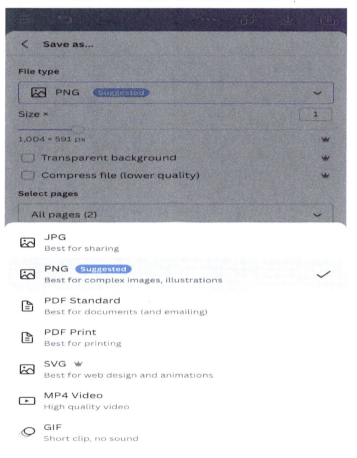

- Explore More Templates: If you need additional templates for different projects or purposes, repeat the process to browse and select more templates from Canva's extensive library.

CREATE A DESIGN

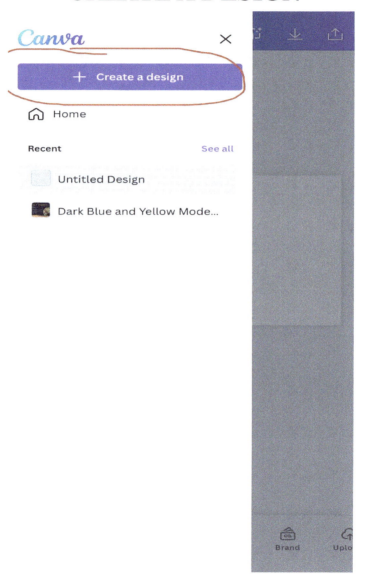

To create designs in Canva, follow these steps:

- **Choose a Template or Start from Scratch:** Begin by selecting a template from Canva's library that matches your project's purpose and style. Alternatively, choose to start with a blank canvas.
- If starting from scratch, you'll be prompted to enter custom dimensions for your canvas or select from popular presets such as social media posts, presentations, posters, etc.

| 🔍 Search | | Cancel |

⟷ Custom size

Suggested

▤ Doc Auto size

▯ Mobile Video 1080 × 1920 px

▤ Document Auto size

▤ Book Cover 1410 × 2250 px

◉ Presentation (16:9) 1920 × 1080 px

▤ Resume 21 × 29.7 cm

▨ Phone Wallpaper 1080 × 1920 px

◉ Instagram Story 1080 × 1920 px

◉ WhatsApp Status 1080 × 1920 px

✉ Card (Landscape) 14.8 × 10.5 cm

▥ Photo Collage (Portrait) 20 × 30 cm

◉ Your Story 1080 × 1920 px

▣ Business Card (Landscape) 8.5 × 5 cm

- **Customize Your Design:** Once you've selected a template or created a blank canvas, customize your design by adding text, images, shapes, and other elements.
- Click on the elements panel on the left side of the screen to access various design elements such as text, photos, grids, shapes, icons, and more.
- Drag and drop elements onto the canvas to add them to your design.

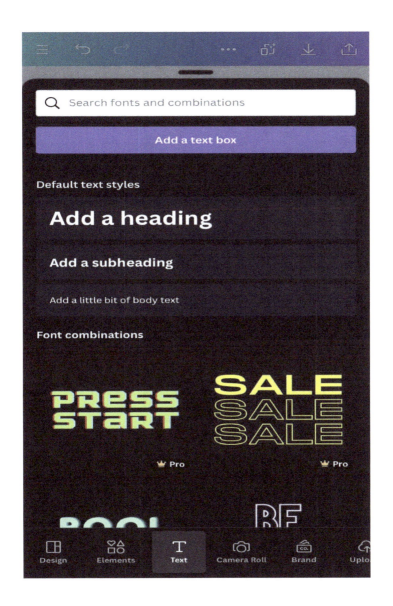

PROMO OFFER

Font ×

Helvetica World >

HEY GOTCHA! ♛

✓ **HORIZON**

Impact

INTRO RUST ♛

ITC Bauhaus >

ITC Benguiat >

PROMO OFFER

⌨	F*f*	H	A**A**	✎	✕
Edit	Font	Text styles	Font size	Col	

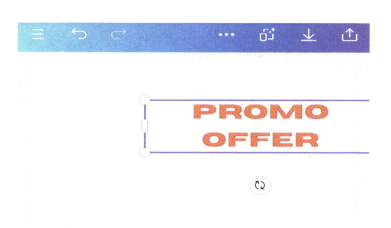

Color   ✕

🎨 **Default colors**

Solid colors

- **Use Drag-and-Drop Functionality:** Canva's drag-and-drop functionality makes it easy to position elements on the canvas exactly where you want them.
- Click on an element to select it, then drag it to move it around the canvas. Release the mouse button to drop the element into place.

- **Customize Design Elements:** Customize colors, fonts, sizes, and other design elements using the toolbar at the top of the screen.
- Click on a text box or shape to select it, then use the toolbar options to change its color, font, size, alignment, and more.
- For images, click on the image to reveal options for adjusting brightness, contrast, saturation, and other image settings.

- **Utilize Layers:** Canva allows you to manage elements' arrangement using layers.
- Each element you add to the canvas is placed on a separate layer, allowing you to easily rearrange them.
- To access layers, click on the "Layers" tab on the right side of the screen. You can drag elements up or down in the layers panel to change their stacking order.

- **Preview and Edit:** Periodically preview your design by zooming out or clicking on the "Preview" button to see how it looks as a whole.
- Make any necessary edits or adjustments to your design by selecting elements and using the editing tools available.

- **Save and Download Your Design:** Once your design is complete, click on the "Download" button to save it to your computer or device.

- Choose the desired file format (e.g., PNG, JPG, PDF) and quality settings before downloading.
- You can also save your design to your Canva account by clicking on the "Save" button to access it later or make further edits.

ADDING IMAGES

To add images to your design in Canva, follow these steps:

- **Access the Photos Tab**: Click on the "Photos" tab located on the left-hand side panel of the Canva interface.

- **Search for Images:** Use the search bar at the top of the Photos tab to enter keywords related to the type of image you're looking for. For example, if you're creating a social media post about travel, you might search for terms like "beach," "mountains," or "adventure."

- **Browse Image Categories:** Scroll down to explore the various categories of images available in Canva's library.

- Categories may include nature, business, food, fashion, travel, and more.

- **Select an Image:** Click on an image thumbnail to select it and add it to your design canvas.
- Alternatively, you can drag and drop an image directly from the Photos tab onto your canvas.

- **Customize Image Settings:** Once the image is added to your canvas, you can resize and reposition it as needed by clicking and dragging the corner handles or the image itself.
- To rotate the image, hover over one of the corner handles until the rotation icon appears, then click and drag to rotate.
- **Replace or Upload Your Own Images:** If you prefer to use your own images instead of those from Canva's library, you can upload them by clicking on the "Uploads" tab in the left-hand side panel.

- Click on the "Upload an image or video" button and select the image file(s) from your computer or device.
- Once uploaded, your images will appear in the Uploads tab, and you can drag and drop them onto your canvas just like Canva's stock images.

- **Adjust Image Properties:** After adding an image to your canvas, you can adjust its properties by clicking on the image to reveal additional options.
- Depending on the image, you may have options to adjust brightness, contrast, saturation, blur, transparency, and more.
- Explore these settings to fine-tune your images and achieve the desired visual effect for your design.

- **Save and Download Your Design:** Once your design is complete, click on the "Download" button to save it to your computer or device.

- Choose the desired file format (e.g., PNG, JPG, PDF) and quality settings before downloading.
- You can also save your design to your Canva account by clicking on the "Save" button to access it later or make further edits.

By following these steps, you can easily add images to your designs in Canva, whether you're using Canva's library of stock photos or uploading your own images. Experiment with different images, layouts, and design elements to create visually appealing and engaging designs for any purpose.

Below are some images for better illustrations.

REMOVING IMAGE BACKGROUND

To remove the background from an image in Canva, you can use the Background Remover tool. Here's how:

Note: Only Canva pro can use this feature

- Select the Image: Start by adding the image to your Canva design canvas. You can either upload your own image or use one from Canva's library.
- Open the Background Remover: Once the image is added to your canvas, click on the image to select it.
- A toolbar will appear at the top of the screen. Click on the "Effects" button (it looks like a magic wand).

- **Use the Background Remover Tool**: In the Effects panel, you'll see various options. Look for the

"Background Remover" tool and click on it.

- Canva will automatically remove the background from the selected image. You'll see the background become transparent.

- **Adjust the Result (Optional):** If needed, you can adjust the result by using the "Adjust" slider under the Background Remover tool.
- Moving the slider to the right will increase the removal intensity, while moving it to the left will decrease it.
- Play around with the slider until you're satisfied with the result.

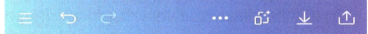

COLLABORATE

Collaborating with others in Canva allows you to work on designs together in real-time, making it easy to share ideas, provide feedback, and collaborate on projects. Here's how to collaborate in Canva:

Share Your Design:

•   Once you've created a design, click on the "Share" button located in the top right corner of the editor.

•   In the sharing options menu, you have several choices:

•   Invite people: Enter the email addresses of the people you want to collaborate with. They will receive an email invitation to view and edit the design.

•   Copy link: Generate a shareable link that you can send to others. Anyone with the link can view and edit the design.

•   Share to social media: Share your design directly to social media platforms like Facebook, Twitter, or LinkedIn.

• Embed: Get an embed code to embed your design on a website or blog.

Collaborate in Real-Time:

• Once you've shared your design, collaborators can access it by clicking on the link in the email invitation or the shareable link you provided.

• All collaborators can work on the design simultaneously in real-time. Changes made by one person are instantly visible to others.

• Collaborators can add or edit text, images, and other elements, as well as leave comments for discussion.

Manage Collaboration:

• As the owner of the design, you can manage collaboration settings and permissions.

• Click on the "Share" button again to access the sharing options menu.

- From here, you can:
- Add or remove collaborators.
- Change collaborators' access permissions (e.g., edit, comment, view only).
- Disable link sharing or revoke access to the design.

Communicate and Provide Feedback:
- Use the comments feature to communicate with collaborators and provide feedback on the design.
- Click on any element in the design and select the "Comment" button to leave a comment. Collaborators can reply to comments and have threaded discussions.

Track Changes:
- Canva automatically tracks changes made by collaborators, allowing you to see who made each change and when.
- Click on the "Show history" button in the editor to view a timeline of edits and revisions.

Save and Download the Final Design:
•   Once the design is complete, you can save and download it as usual.
•   Click on the "Download" button to save the design to your computer in the desired file format.

By collaborating in Canva, you can harness the collective creativity and expertise of your team or collaborators to create stunning designs together efficiently and effectively.

LEARN AND EXPLORE

To learn and explore more in Canva, you can take advantage of various resources and features available within the platform:

Canva Design School:
• Explore the Canva Design School, which offers a wealth of tutorials, courses, and resources to help you improve your design skills.
• Access the Design School from the Canva website by clicking on the "Learn" tab in the top navigation menu.
• Learn about design principles, typography, color theory, branding, and more through interactive tutorials and articles.

Tutorials and Guides:
• Canva provides step-by-step tutorials and guides to help you master different aspects of design.

• Explore the tutorials section in the Canva Design School or visit the Canva Help Center for in-depth guides and troubleshooting tips.

Design Tips and Inspiration:

• Follow Canva's social media channels and blog for design tips, inspiration, and creative ideas.

• Connect with the Canva community by joining design-related groups and forums to share ideas and learn from others.

Explore Templates and Elements:

• Take time to explore Canva's vast library of templates, graphics, photos, and other design elements.

• Experiment with different template categories, styles, and layouts to discover new design possibilities.

• Customize existing templates to suit your needs, or create your own designs from scratch using Canva's elements.

Try New Features:

• Stay updated on new features and updates released by Canva.

• Keep an eye out for feature announcements and release notes to learn about new tools and functionalities that can enhance your design workflow.

Attend Workshops and Webinars:

• Participate in workshops, webinars, and online events hosted by Canva or industry experts.

• These events provide valuable insights, tips, and techniques to help you level up your design skills and stay current with industry trends.

Practice and Experiment:

• The best way to learn and improve in Canva is through practice and experimentation.

• Set aside time to create new designs, try out different techniques, and push the boundaries of your creativity.

- Don't be afraid to make mistakes, as they often lead to valuable learning experiences.

TUTORIALS ON CREATING DESIGNS

<u>Sample 1 (Instagram post)</u>

Creating an Instagram post design in Canva is simple and straightforward. Follow these step-by-step instructions to create a visually appealing Instagram post:

- **Choose Instagram Post Template:** In the search bar at the top of the page, type "Instagram post" and press Enter.
- Select the "Instagram Post" template from the search results. Canva offers various Instagram post templates with different layouts and styles.

- **Customize Template:** Once you've selected a template, you'll be taken to the Canva editor where you can customize the design.
- Replace the placeholder text with your own caption or message. Click on the text box to edit the text and adjust the font, size, and color using the editing toolbar at the top of the screen.

- If you want to add additional text, click on the "Text" tab on the left-hand side panel to access more text options and drag them onto the canvas.

- **Add Images:** To add images to your Instagram post, click on the "Photos" tab on the left-hand side panel.
- Browse through the available photos or use the search bar to find specific images. Drag the desired image onto the canvas to add it to your design.
- You can also upload your own images by clicking on the "Uploads" tab and selecting the image file from your computer or device.
- Alternatively, you can replace the image on the post with your desired image from your gallery.

Or click on the element icon then search for the image you want to use and then select one from the graphic or photo options.

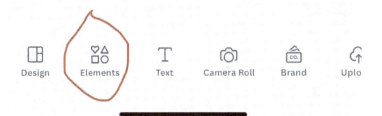

- Click on the image you want to reposition to select it. You'll know it's selected when it's surrounded by a bounding box with selection handles.
- **Access the Positioning Options**: Once the image is selected, you'll see a toolbar at the top of the screen. Look for the "Position" option in the toolbar. It usually looks like a square

with an arrow pointing upwards and downwards.

- **Send Backward:** Click on the "Position" option, and a drop-down menu will appear. From the menu, select the "Send backward" or "Move backward" option. This will move the image one layer backward, placing it behind other elements on the canvas.

- **Repeat if Necessary:** If you want the image to go further backward, you can repeat the process by selecting the image again and choosing "Send backward" or "Move backward" from the "Position" menu.

- **Adjust as Needed:** After repositioning the image, you can further adjust its position by clicking and dragging it on the canvas. This allows you to precisely place the image relative to other elements in your design.

Position   ×

⬍ Forward   ⬍ Backward

⬍ To front   ⬍ To back

Arrange   Align   Advanced

- Customize the layout and elements of your design by clicking and dragging them to reposition or resize them.
- Experiment with different backgrounds, colors, and graphic elements to enhance the visual appeal of your Instagram post.
- You can also add shapes, icons, stickers, or illustrations from the "Elements" tab to further personalize your design.
- To move an image or text, you can use the nudge icon or select, pick and drop the image to the preferred location.

Nudge ✕

 Design   Elements   Text   Camera Roll   Brand   Uplo

- **Preview and Finalize:** Once you're satisfied with your Instagram post design, click on the "Preview" button to see how it will look on Instagram.

- Make any final adjustments or edits as needed.
- When you're ready, click on the "Download" button to save your Instagram post design to your computer or device.

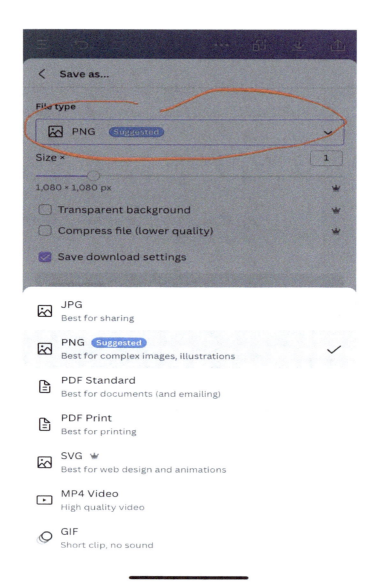

JPG
Best for sharing

PNG **Suggested** ✓
Best for complex images, illustrations

PDF Standard
Best for documents (and emailing)

PDF Print
Best for printing

SVG 👑
Best for web design and animations

MP4 Video
High quality video

GIF
Short clip, no sound

- **Post on Instagram:** After downloading your design, you can upload it to your Instagram account as a new post.
- Open the Instagram app on your mobile device, tap the "+" icon at the bottom of the screen, select "Feed," and choose the downloaded image from your camera roll.
- Write a caption, add hashtags if desired, and click on "Share" to publish your Instagram post.

Sample 2 (Book Cover)

Follow these step-by-step instructions to design a professional-looking book cover:

- **Choose Book Cover Template:** In the search bar at the top of the page, type "book cover" and press Enter.
- Select the "Book Cover" template from the search results. Canva offers a variety of book cover templates in different styles and genres.

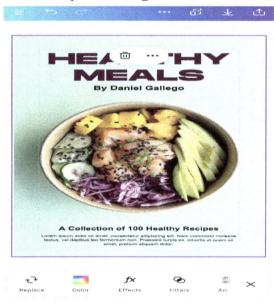

- **Customize Template:** Once you've selected a template, you'll be taken to the Canva editor where you can customize the design. Change background color if necessary.

- Replace the placeholder text with your own title, subtitle, and author name. Click on the text box to edit the text and adjust the font, size, and color using the editing toolbar at the top of the screen.
- If you want to add additional text, click on the "Text" tab on the left-hand side panel to access more text options and drag them onto the canvas.

- **Add Images:** To add images to your book cover, click on the "Photos" tab on the left-hand side panel.
- Browse through the available photos or use the search bar to find specific images. Drag the desired image onto the canvas to add it to your design.
- You can also upload your own images by clicking on the "Uploads" tab and selecting the image file from your computer or device.

- **Adjust Layout and Elements:** Customize the layout and elements of your book cover design by clicking and dragging them to reposition or resize them.
- Experiment with different backgrounds, colors, and graphic elements to enhance the visual appeal of your book cover.
- You can also add shapes, icons, stickers, or illustrations from the "Elements" tab to further personalize your design.

HEALTHY MEALS

By Daniel Gallego

A Collection of 100 Healthy Recipes

Lorem ipsum dolor sit amet, consectetur adipiscing elit. Nam commodo molestie lectus, vel dapibus leo fermentum non. Praesent turpis ex, lobortis at quam sit amet, pretium aliquam dolor.

Edit	Font	Text styles	Font size	Col	×

Font size   ✕

Font size   120

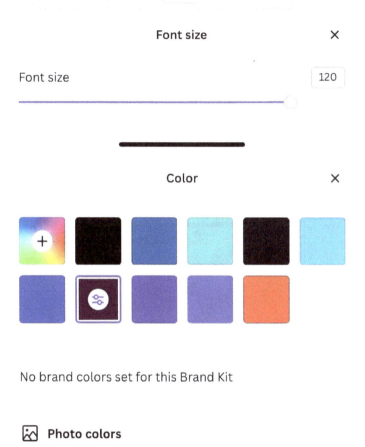

Color   ✕

No brand colors set for this Brand Kit

🖼 **Photo colors**

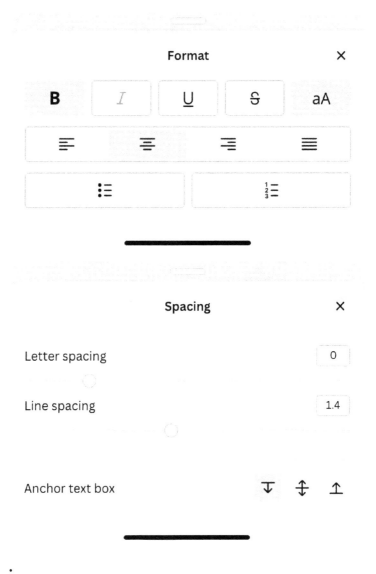

Format   ✕

B   *I*   U̲   S̸   aA

Spacing   ✕

Letter spacing   0

Line spacing   1.4

Anchor text box

Animate   ✕

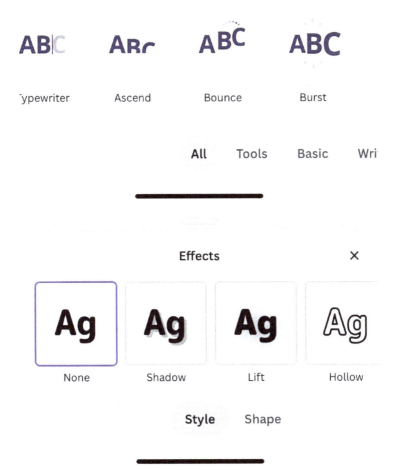

ypewriter   Ascend   Bounce   Burst

All   Tools   Basic   Wri

Effects   ✕

None   Shadow   Lift   Hollow

Style   Shape

HEALTHY

By Daniel Gallego

A Collection of 100 Healthy Recipes

Lorem ipsum dolor sit amet, consectetur adipiscing elit. Nam commodo molestie lectus, vel dapibus leo fermentum non. Praesent turpis ex, lobortis at quam sit amet, pretium aliquam dolor.

Transparency   ✕

Transparency   20

- **Preview and Finalize:** Once you're satisfied with your book cover design, click on the "Preview" button to see how it will look as a finished product.
- Make any final adjustments or edits as needed.
- When you're ready, click on the "Download" button to save your book cover design to your computer or device.

- **Print or Publish:** After downloading your design, you can print it out if you plan to use it for a physical book cover.
- If you're publishing an e-book, you can upload the cover image to your publishing platform along with your book manuscript.

Sample 3 (Resume)

- **Choose Resume Template:**

In the search bar at the top of the page, type "resume" and press Enter.

• Select the "Resume" template category from the search results. Canva offers a variety of resume templates in different styles and formats.

- **Select Template:**

• Browse through the available resume templates and choose one that aligns with your industry, experience level, and personal style.

• Canva offers templates for various types of resumes, including chronological, functional, and combination formats.

- **Customize Template:**

• Once you've selected a template, you'll be taken to the Canva editor where you can customize the design.

• Replace the placeholder text with your own information, including your name, contact information, work experience, education, skills, and any other relevant details.

• Click on the text boxes to edit the text and adjust the font, size, and color using the editing toolbar at the top of the screen.

- **Add Sections:**

• Customize the layout and content of your resume by adding or removing sections as needed.

• Canva offers a variety of section templates that you can drag and drop onto your resume, such as work experience, education, skills, certifications, and awards.

- **Customize Design:**

• Customize the design of your resume by changing the colors, fonts, and background elements to match your personal brand or desired aesthetic.

• Experiment with different color schemes, fonts, and graphic elements to create a unique and visually appealing resume design.

- **Add Images or Icons:**
• Enhance your resume design by adding images or icons that represent your skills, interests, or achievements.
• Canva offers a wide range of images, icons, and illustrations that you can drag and drop onto your resume to personalize it further.

- **Preview and Finalize:**
• Once you're satisfied with your resume design, click on the "Preview" button to see how it will look as a finished product.
• Make any final adjustments or edits as needed.
• When you're ready, click on the "Download" button to save your resume design to your computer or device.

- **Use Your Resume:**

•   After downloading your resume design, you can use it to apply for jobs by printing it out or sending it electronically to potential employers.

•   You can also save your resume design as a PDF and upload it to job search websites or attach it to email applications.

Sample 4 (Logo)

- **Choose Logo Template:**
• In the search bar at the top of the page, type "logo" and press Enter.
• Select the "Logo" template category from the search results. Canva offers a variety of logo templates in different styles and industries.

- **Explore Templates:**
• Browse through the available logo templates and choose one that aligns with your brand's style, personality, and industry.
• Canva offers templates for various types of logos, including wordmark logos, emblem logos, icon logos, and combination logos.

- **Customize Template:**
• Once you've selected a template, you'll be taken to the Canva editor where you can customize the design.

• Replace the placeholder text with your own brand name or initials. Click on the text box to edit the text and adjust the font, size, and color using the editing toolbar at the top of the screen.

• If the template includes graphic elements or icons, you can customize them by changing their colors, sizes, and positions on the canvas.

- **Add or Edit Elements:**

• Customize the layout and elements of your logo design by clicking and dragging them to reposition or resize them.

• Experiment with different shapes, lines, icons, and illustrations from the "Elements" tab to create a unique and memorable logo.

• You can also add additional text, shapes, or decorative elements to enhance your logo design.

- **Adjust Colors and Effects:**
  - Customize the colors and effects of your logo design to match your brand's color scheme and aesthetic.
  - Click on any element in your design to reveal options for changing its color, opacity, shadow, or other effects.
  - Experiment with different color combinations and effects until you achieve the desired look for your logo.

- **Preview and Finalize:**
  - Once you're satisfied with your logo design, click on the "Preview" button to see how it will look in different contexts.
  - Make any final adjustments or edits as needed.
  - When you're ready, click on the "Download" button to save your logo design to your computer or device.

- **Use Your Logo:**
  - After downloading your logo design, you can use it across various

platforms and materials to represent your brand.

•   Use your logo on your website, social media profiles, business cards, stationery, packaging, and other marketing materials to create a cohesive brand identity.

Sample 5 (poster)

- Choose Poster Template:

• In the search bar at the top of the page, type "poster" and press Enter.

• Select the "Poster" template category from the search results. Canva offers a variety of poster templates in different styles and sizes.

- Select Template:

• Browse through the available poster templates and choose one that aligns with the purpose and theme of your poster.

• Canva offers templates for various types of posters, including event posters, promotional posters, educational posters, and more.

- Customize Template:

• Once you've selected a template, you'll be taken to the Canva editor where you can customize the design.

• Replace the placeholder text with your own message, information, or content. Click on the text boxes to edit the text and adjust the font, size, and color using the editing toolbar at the top of the screen.

• Customize the layout and elements of your poster design by clicking and dragging them to reposition or resize them.

- **Add Images or Graphics:**
• Enhance your poster design by adding images, graphics, or illustrations that complement your message or theme.

• Click on the "Photos" tab on the left-hand side panel to access Canva's library of stock photos. Drag the desired image onto the canvas to add it to your design.

• You can also upload your own images or graphics by clicking on the "Uploads" tab and selecting the image file from your computer or device.

- Customize Design Elements:

• Customize the colors, fonts, and backgrounds of your poster design to match your theme or branding.

• Click on any element in your design to reveal options for changing its color, opacity, shadow, or other effects.

• Experiment with different color schemes, fonts, and graphic elements until you achieve the desired look for your poster.

- Preview and Finalize:

• Once you're satisfied with your poster design, click on the "Preview" button to see how it will look as a finished product.

• Make any final adjustments or edits as needed.

• When you're ready, click on the "Download" button to save your poster design to your computer or device.

- **Print or Share Your Poster:**

    • After downloading your poster design, you can print it out if you plan to display it in a physical location.

    • You can also share your poster design electronically by uploading it to social media, emailing it to friends or colleagues, or embedding it on a website or blog.

Sample 6 (Journal)

Creating a journal design in Canva allows you to customize every aspect of your journal, from the cover to the interior pages. Follow these step-by-step instructions to design a journal:

- **Choose Journal Template:**
    • In the search bar at the top of the page, type "journal" and press Enter.
    • Select the "Journal" template category from the search results. Canva offers a variety of journal templates in different styles and layouts.

- **Select Template:**
    • Browse through the available journal templates and choose one that fits your preferences and needs.
    • Canva offers templates for various types of journals, including lined journals, blank journals, bullet journals, and more.

- **Customize Cover:**
    • Once you've selected a template, you'll be taken to the Canva editor where you can customize the design.
    • Replace the placeholder text on the cover with your own title, subtitle, and any other text you want to include. Click on the text box to edit the text and adjust the font, size, and color using the editing toolbar.
    • Customize the cover design by adding images, graphics, or illustrations that reflect the theme or purpose of your journal. You can use Canva's library of stock photos and graphics or upload your own images.

- **Design Interior Pages:**
    • Customize the layout and design of the interior pages of your journal. You can create lined pages, blank pages, grid pages, or any other type of layout you prefer.
    • Use the text tool to add headings, prompts, or other text elements to

your pages. You can also add decorative elements, such as borders, dividers, or illustrations, to enhance the visual appeal of your journal.

- **Add Personal Touches:**
    • Make your journal design unique and personal by adding custom elements that reflect your personality or interests.
    • Experiment with different colors, fonts, and graphic styles to create a design that feels authentic to you.
    • You can also add quotes, images, or other meaningful elements that inspire or motivate you.

- **Preview and Finalize:**
    • Once you're satisfied with your journal design, click on the "Preview" button to see how it will look as a finished product.
    • Make any final adjustments or edits as needed.

• When you're ready, click on the "Download" button to save your journal design to your computer or device.

- **Print Your Journal:**

• After downloading your journal design, you can print it out if you plan to use it as a physical journal.

• You can print the cover and interior pages separately and bind them together, or you can print them together as a complete journal.